GET YOUR BIBLE OUT OF THE SADDLE BAG!

Volume One: Genesis through Esther

CHARLES HIGGS & GREG LONG

WESTBOW
PRESS
A DIVISION OF THOMAS NELSON

WestBow Press books may be ordered through booksellers or by contacting:

WestBow Press
A Division of Thomas Nelson
1663 Liberty Drive
Bloomington, IN 47403
www.westbowpress.com
1-(866) 928-1240

Because of the dynamic nature of the Internet, any web addresses or links contained in
this book may have changed since publication and may no longer be valid. The views
expressed in this work are solely those of the author and do not necessarily reflect the
views of the publisher, and the publisher hereby disclaims any responsibility for them.

Any people depicted in stock imagery provided by Thinkstock are models,
and such images are being used for illustrative purposes only.

Certain stock imagery © Thinkstock.

ISBN: 978-1-4497-3081-9 (sc)
ISBN: 978-1-4497-3080-2 (e)

Library of Congress Control Number: 2011960333

Printed in the United States of America

WestBow Press rev. date: 11/17/2011

TABLE OF CONTENTS

PREFACE

The Harvest Field of the Western Heritage is white unto harvest and we praise the Lord in what He is doinq in the Cowboy Churches across America. One of the urgent needs of the Cowboy Church is Bible Study/Discipleship helps. I have teamed up with Dr. Greg Long, Pastor of Lost Pines Cowboy Church of Elgin, Texas, to write a six volume study book called "Get that Bible out of Your Saddlebag!" Each lesson is a digest/summary of each Book of the Bible.

Volume One: Genesis thru Esther

Volume Two: Covers the Four Gospels: Acts, Romans, Letters of James, John, Peter, Jude and the Book of Hebrews

Volume Three: Job, Psalms, Proverbs, Ecclesiastes, Song of Solomon, and Lamentations

Volume Four: Paul's Writings & Letters

Volume Five: Old Testament Minor & Major Prophets

Volume Six: Revelation . . . The Big Rodeo & God Wins!

It is our desire to see the other five volumes published in the next few years.

There are study notes for the leader of the Bible Study.

Go to *www.texasbaptists.org* and click Western Heritage and you will finds the study helps on that page.

So "*Get That Bible Out of Your Saddlebag*" and ride the trail with us!

See You on the Trail!

Charles Higgs . . . Director of Western Heritage Ministry of Texas Baptist

LESSON ONE: GENESIS

"In the beginning God created the heavens and the earth."
Genesis 1:1 KJV

Genesis pictures "Christ the Creator!"
Genesis means "in the beginning." This book was authored by Moses and was probably written 1445-1405 B.C.

Creation: Chapters 1-2
God created everything out of nothing. He made all of this for you and me. He created the first man, Adam, and the first woman, Eve, and placed them in the Garden of Eden.

The Fall and the Results of the Fall: Chapters (3-5)
A Little Humor: *Adam was walking with his sons Cain and Abel. They passed by the ruins of the Garden of Eden. One of the boys asked, "What's that?" Adam replied, "Boys, that's where your mother ate us out of house and home."*

The fall of man was not a funny thing because we are still dealing with the aftermath. Satan interrupted God's great plan for humanity by tempting and convincing Adam and Eve to disobey God.

We look at the first prophecy and see how God will redeem humanity. *"I'm declaring war between you and the Woman, between your offspring and hers. He'll wound your head, you'll wound his heel."* Genesis 3:15—The Message

The aftermath of the fall of men is that the descendants follow the path of violence, wickedness, and immorality.

Here Comes the Flood and a New Start (6-11)

Humanity became so sinful that God had to destroy humanity though a worldwide flood. Noah, a righteous man, and his family were saved by preparing an ark. Noah's family would replenish the earth.

Father Abraham had Many Sons (12-25)

God called a man named Abram whom he renamed Abraham. He left his homeland and traveled to a new land. He became the Father of the Jews. He was 100 and his wife Sarah was in her 90's when their first son, Isaac, was born. Abraham's greatest descendant would be Jesus Christ. (Matthew 1)

Isaac and his Two Sons (24-28)

Isaac, whose name means laughter, had two sons, Jacob and Esau. Isaac received his name when Abraham, who was one hundred, fell on the floor laughing when He was told by God that his wife Sarah, who was in her nineties, would conceive a son. Jacob, whose name means "manipulator", manipulated his father's blessing from his father Isaac.

Jacob Becomes Israel (28-36)

Jacob left home and while sleeping on the ground had a dream. In the dream he saw himself wrestling with God. God gave Jacob the name of "Israel" which means "struggling with God." Jacob had twelve sons which gave birth to the twelve tribes of Israel.

Joseph the Dreamer & God Knows the Rest of the Story (37-50) The man who went from a "Pit to the Palace." Joseph's story would have been a good *"Now You Know the Rest of the Story"*, that the late Paul Harvey could have used. Joseph was Jacob's favorite son. His brothers became jealous and sold Joseph into slavery. After 17 years of trials Joseph became Prime Minister of Egypt. He forgave his brothers and brought Jacob and all the family to Egypt to live. Joseph was a great administrator and saved two nations from disaster.

Apply Genesis to your life
God took ordinary people and did extraordinary things through them. Noah, Abraham, Jacob, Joseph, and others made a difference for God. You too can make a difference for God's Kingdom. You fit into God's purpose just like they did. They allowed God to work in their lives and we must allow God to work in our lives.

Lesson to learn from Genesis
1. You are made in the image of God.
2. God uses imperfect people to accomplish His purpose.
3. God is Sovereign.
4. God rejects sin and disobedience.
5. God is always ready to turn our trials into triumph.

Find it in Genesis

- Creation (1:1-2:3)
- First Prophecy (3:15)
- Noah and the Ark (6-8)

- Abraham's willingness to sacrifice Isaac (22)
- Joseph interprets Pharaoh's Dream (41)

One of the Legends from Genesis Abraham
- Married his half sister Sarah
- Rescued his nephew Lot
- His name meant "Father of Multitudes"
- He was a friend of God (2 Chronicles 20:7)
- He lived 175 Years
- He is listed in "God's Hall of Faith" (Hebrews 11)

One of the Legends from the Western Heritage Culture Charles Badger Clark (1883-1957)

Charles Badger Clark is the most revered name in Cowboy poetry. He was born in Iowa but grew up in South Dakota. Clark migrated to the Southwest and ranched in Arizona. He learned that he could sell and perform his poetry so he traded his saddle for a pen. His most famous poem was "The Cowboy Prayer."

> Oh Lord, I've never lived where churches grow.
> I loved creation better as it stood
> That day You finished it so long ago
> And looked upon Your work and called it good.
> That stretches upward toward the Great Divide."
> —Charles Badger Clark

LESSON TWO: EXODUS

"I have come down to deliver them out of the hand of Egyptians, and bring them up from that land to a good and large land." Exodus 3:8 ASV

Exodus pictures "Christ the Passover Lamb!"
Exodus was authored by Moses and written 1445-1405 B.C. This book covers the Israelites exodus and journey from Egypt to Mount Sinai.

Get me out of here! Chapters 1-6
God heard the cry from the suffering Israelites. He sent Moses and prepared him for the task of leading the Israelites out of Egypt. D.L. Moody once said, *"It is an interesting story of how God prepared Moses"*.

Let my people go! Chapters 7-18
It took ten dramatic plagues for Moses to convince Pharaoh to let God's people leave Egypt, including the plague of the death of the first born. Pharaoh finally released the Israelites but later had a change of heart and pursued them. God divided the Red Sea so the Israelites could escape. He then closed the Red Sea and Pharaoh and the Egyptian Army drown. God's people who were delivered from Pharaoh and Egypt found that God would feed and

take care of all their physical needs. Soon they forgot about the blessings of God.

Think about this!
The Israelites numbered from 2 to 3 million people. "There were about six hundred thousand men on foot plus the women and children." (12:38) God led them and fed them. Moses had his challenges and difficulties in leading such a great host of people.

The Big 10! Chapters 19:1-24:8
Three months after leaving Egypt they arrived at Mount Sinai. It is there that God made a covenant with them that they would be "a kingdom of priests and a holy nation" (19:6). The ground rules were stipulated on what we know as the "Ten Commandments." (20:1-17) There were other laws dealing with civil affairs and sacred observances given in chapters 21-23. The covenant was ratified by the blood (24:1-8)

The Ten Commandments

ONE: *'You shall have no other gods before Me.'*

TWO: *'You shall not make for yourself a carved image—*
          any likeness of anything that is in heaven above,
          or that is in the earth beneath, or that is in the
          water under the earth.'

THREE: *'You shall not take the name of the LORD your*
          God in vain.'

FOUR: *'Remember the Sabbath day, to keep it holy.'*

FIVE: *'Honor your father and your mother.'*

SIX: *'You shall not murder.'*

SEVEN: *'You shall not commit adultery.'*

EIGHT: *'You shall not steal.'*

NINE: 'You shall not bear false witness against your neighbor.'

TEN: 'You shall not covet your neighbor's house; you shall not covet your neighbor's wife, nor his male servant, nor his female servant, nor his ox, nor his donkey, nor anything that is your neighbors.'

THE COWBOY'S TEN COMMANDMENTS

1—Just one God.
2—Honor yer Ma & Pa.
3—No telling tales or gossipin'.
4—Git yourself to Sunday meeting.
5—Put nothin' before God.
6—No foolin' around with another fellow's gal.
7—No killin'.
8—Watch yer mouth.
9—Don't take what ain't yers.
10—Don't be hankerin' for yer buddy's stuff

The Big Tent! (24:9 thru 40:38)

Moses returned to the top of Mount Sinai. God gave him instruction concerning the moveable tabernacle, a portable building or tent, which would be used for worship. During this time God punished Israel for idolatry because they had erected the golden calf and worshiped it. A year after the Exodus the building of the Tabernacle was completed.

Learn from this

- God heard their cry and He hears your cry for help.
- Moses tried to use excuses to escape God's call upon his life. God does not want our excuses He wants us.

- The first four commandments deals with our relationship with God. The last six concerns our relationship with humanity.

I see Jesus in Exodus
- I see Jesus in the Passover Lamb. (Exodus 12 & I Corinthians 5:7)
- I see Jesus as our manna in the wilderness. (Exodus16 & John 6:32-35)
- I see Jesus in our High Priest. (Exodus 28 & Hebrews 5:4-5)
- I see Jesus as our Tabernacle. (Exodus 25 & John 1:14)

Will Rogers, The Cowboy Philosopher, gave his opinion about the 10 Commandments:
"*Whoever wrote the Ten Commandments made'em short. They may not always be kept but they are understood.*"

Relating to the Big Ten
Number 1: My main priority is to please God.

Number 2: I need to accept God as He is and not cut Him down to my size.

Number 3: I need to honor Him in my daily life.

Number 4: Make my worship special to Him.

Number 5: I must Honor my parents and family.

Number 6: I must respect human life.

Number 7: I need to be faithful to my spouse.

Number 8: I need to be careful about other people's property and processions.

Number 9: I need to practice honesty in everything.

Number 10: I need to be content and thankful for what I have.

The Legend of Exodus is Moses

Moses was a great hero of God. D.L. Moody said that Moses spent:

Forty years thinking he was **somebody**
Forty years learning that he was a **nobody**
Forty years discovering what God can do with a **nobody**

The Legend from Western Heritage Past
Gene Autry

Gene was born in Tioga, Texas, on September 29, 1907. His father was a horse trader and livestock dealer. His grandfather was a Baptist Minister and taught him to sing. When he was eight years old he bought his first guitar from a Sears & Roebuck Catalog. In the 1920's Will Rogers encouraged young Autry to try radio and the rest is history. Gene Autry recorded many great songs including "I'm Back in the Saddle Again." He also played in many western movies. He produced 91 half-hour episodes of the Gene Autry Show. He was past owner of the California Angels and at one time served as Vice-President of the American League. Gene Autry died in 1998.

The Cowboy Code by Gene Autry

1. The cowboy must never shoot first, hit a smaller man, or take unfair advantage.
2. He must never go back on his word or a trust confided in him.
3. He must always tell the truth.
4. He must be gentle with children, the elderly, and animals.

5. He must not advocate or possess racially or religiously intolerant ideas.
6. He must help people in distress.
7. He must be a good worker.
8. He must keep himself clean in thought, speech, action, and personal habits.
9. He must respect women, parents, and his nation's laws.
10. The Cowboy is a patriot.

LESSON THREE: LEVITICUS

"I am the Lord your God . . . you shall be holy; for I am holy." Leviticus 11:44 NKJV 1983

Leviticus pictures "Christ as our Sacrifice!

It had been one year since God's people left Egypt. The tabernacle had been constructed and was now in use. As Leviticus begins the Israelites are still camping at the base of Mt. Sinai in the wilderness. More instructions on worship were needed. In this book we find what God expected in the observances of feast and sacrifices.

The Laws of Worship: Chapters 1-7

There would be five types of sacrifices:

- Burnt Offering "Surrender"
- Meal Offering "Service"
- Peace Offering "Serenity"
- Sin Offering "Substitute for Sins of the people"
- Trespass Offering "Satisfying God's demands.

The Laws of Priesthood: Chapters 8-10

Tells how the priest should carry out their priestly duties.

The Laws of Standards and Daily Living: Chapters 11-16
These laws deal with what was holy and clean and what was unclean and unholy.

Feast & Festivities that are Important to God & His People
- Feast of the Sabbath—23:1-3
- Feast of the Passover—23:4-5 & Unleavened Bread-23:6-8
- Feast of First Fruits—23:9-14 & Pentecost-23:15-22
- Feast of the Trumpets-23:23-25
- The Day Atonement—23:26-32
- The Feast of Tabernacles-23:33-36
- The Sabbatical Year-25:1-7
- The Year of Jubilee-25:8-55

In Genesis we see: Humanity Ruined
In Exodus we see: Humanity Redeemed
In Leviticus we see: Humanity Worshipping

The Number Seven in Exodus
Every 7th day was the Sabbath. Every 7th year was a Sabbatical year. Seven times seven years was followed by a year of Jubilee. In the 7th month were feasts of trumpets, tabernacles, and atonement.

Pentecost was seven weeks after Passover. Pentecost lasted seven days. Passover lasted seven days. Revelation is another book that is built around a series of seven.

Think about it
God is a Holy God and wants us to live a holy life.
Worship tells us that it is not all about us. It is all about HIM.
God loves and expects obedience.

The Legend from Leviticus is Aaron

Aaron was the brother to Moses and was named the first High Priest. Aaron is known for his role as the first high priest. In Old Testament times the high priest was the one that represented people before God. We also know that before he was high priest Aaron was the spokesman for his brother, Moses. God knew that Aaron could 'speak well' and Moses was 'slow of speech'. So Aaron spoke for Moses when they represented God before Pharaoh. Aaron also performed many miracles with Moses that we read about in the Book of Exodus. Aaron was 83 years old when he and Moses spoke for God to Pharaoh. They told him that God wanted his people, the Israelites, to be freed from Egypt so they could worship God in the desert. Pharaoh would not listen and many plagues showing God's power came upon Egypt until he finally let God's people go. These are referred to as the 10 plagues and can be found in Exodus 7-12.

Although Aaron was a good man he made some bad choices which made God angry such as making a golden calf, an idol, for the people to worship while Moses was on Mount Sinai (Exodus 32:5). He also shared in Moses' sin at Meribah when Moses struck a rock to get water for the people instead of speaking to the rock as he had been commanded by God. Aaron died on Mount Hor. His robes, which the high priest wore, were taken and given to his son Eleazar who became the next high priest. Moses, his brother, and Eleazar, his son, was present at Aaron's death and buried him. The entire Israelite community mourned his death for 30 days. (Numbers 20: 22-29)

Western Legend
Louis L' Armour

Popular American writer of Westerns, L'Amour was the most significant writer of the genre since the 1950s. His publishing numbers surpassed Frederick Faust (Max Brand), while his popularity rivaled Zane Grey. Hailed on one book cover as the 'World's Greatest Writer', L'Amour sold over 225 million copies, making him the third top-seller in the world (according to *Saturday Review*). L'Amour's books have been translated into dozens of languages and made into 30 films.

"I am probably the last writer who will ever have known the people who lived the frontier life. In drifting about across the West, I have known five men and two women who knew Billy the Kid, two who rode in the Tonto Basin War in Arizona, and a variety of others who were outlaws, or frontier marshals like Jeff Milton, Bill Tilghman, and Chris Madse, or just pioneers."
(from Education of a Wandering Man, 1989)

L'Amour was born in Jamestown, North Dakota. The family name was originally L'Moore or Larmour, reflecting his French-Canadian background. His father had many occupations, including a salesman of farm machinery, a veterinarian, a police chief, and a teacher. L'Amour's mother was trained as a teacher, and she was also an amateur poet. The future author was raised hearing stories of pioneers and Native Americans. He began reading earlier than most—from his parent's bookshelf he found collections of Longfellow, Whittier, Lowell, and Emerson. All the family had library cards.

From the ages of fifteen to nineteen L'Amour worked at a variety of jobs: he tried boxing, worked as a circus hand, a lumberjack, and a seaman, and travelled in the Far East, China, and Africa. He was even an elephant handler for a while. During the 1930s he became a successful boxer and travelled in Asia. After returning to the United States he took some creative writing courses at the University of Oklahoma.

In 1981 L'Amour was one of the five best-selling authors still working, in company with Harold Robbins, Barbara Cartland, Irving Wallace, and Janet Dailey. He reached a wider audience for western stories than any of the other great names: Zane Grey, Max Brand, or Ernest Haycox.

At the time of his death it was estimated that L'Amour had published 101 novels, short story collections, poetry and non-fiction. In spite of his reputation as the ultimate western storywriter, L'Amour's first book, published in 1939, was a collection of poems. Several of his novels were also adapted for the screen. L'Amour was an avid reader and in EDUCATION OF A WANDERING MAN (1989) he gives a colorful picture of his adventurous early years, which were also years of reading. **"Books are the building blocks of civilization, for without the written word, a man knows nothing beyond what occurs during his own brief years and, perhaps, in a few tales his parents tell him.**

Lesson Four: Numbers

"Because all these men who have seen My glory and the signs, which I did in the wilderness, and have put Me to the test now these ten times, and have not heeded My voice, they certainly shall not see the land of which I swore to their fathers, nor shall any of those who rejected Me see it." Numbers 14:22-23 NKJV 1983

Numbers pictures "Christ as the Lifted up One!"

Why call this book "Numbers?"
Twice in this book the people were numbered and counted. (Chapters 1 and 26) This book was also written by Moses around 1445-1440 B.C. It was written in the final year of Moses' life. The Book of Numbers summarizes the events that took place in the second and fortieth years after he lead the Israelites out of Egypt.

Getting Ready to Get On the Trail from Sinai: Chapters 1-10:10
The challenge of leading and feeding three million people was overwhelming to Moses.

God gave them a cloud by day and a pillar of fire by night to guide them.

Blazing the Trail to Kadesh Barnea & Canaan: 10:11-20

- There is quail from God (11:4-35)
- Opposition to Moses (12)
- God's plan rejected (13:26-14:45)
- Korah's Rebellion (16)
- Water from the rock & the bronze serpent (20)
- Joshua succeeds Moses (27)

In Numbers we see the misery of the people and the mercy of God.

Twelve spies from Israel were sent on a mission to spy out the promise land. They returned and ten said that it could not be done and two said that they could possess the land. The negative report became contagious and doubt captivated the people's thinking. They focused on the size of their problem and not the size of their God. God's judgment was that all adults 20 years and older were sentenced to die in the wilderness. Only Joshua and Caleb, the two spies who gave the positive report about possessing the land, would live to enter the land.

A New Day & a New Generation: 21-26

A new census was taken with the second generation who met the challenge of possessing the land. Instructions were given and new challenges were realized. Joshua, the new leader, was chosen to succeed Moses. Joshua would be the one that would lead the Israelites to the Promise Land.

Think and Apply:

The Book of Numbers describes the journey of people who had been redeemed and delivered from Egypt. There is a great lesson for today's Christian. It exactly corresponds to the situation of the Christian in this age. Christians have been redeemed through the blood of Christ and have left Egypt (Bondage of Sin). Christians have been brought out from the control of the powers of sin and of darkness and is headed toward Canaan the Spirit Filled Life.

There is still a rest awaiting the people of God. We are pushing forward toward the rest. The Christian is on a pilgrim journey. He is pressing forward to the great prize ahead of him. This was exactly the situation of the Israelites in the Book of Numbers. No other Book of the Old Testament contains so much that is exactly parallel to the pilgrim journey of today's believers.

Lesson Application: What giant are you facing? Who is bigger—God or your problem?
Fear is caused by not believing what God has told you to do. "God did not give you the spirit of fear . . ."
(2 Tim. 1:7)

When we doubt the plan of God there are consequences.

We have two choices—You can either let fear and panic set in just as the Israelites did and lose your one and only chance to enter into your Promised Land or you can have the same strong faith and belief in God as Joshua and Caleb.

I'll leave you with one last thought. Joshua and Caleb took their strong faith and belief in God, entered the Promised Land, and achieved total victory in God. The Bible says that God is no respecter of persons. What He will do for one, He will do for another.

The Noted Benediction from the Book of Numbers . . . Recognize it?

The Lord bless you and keep you; the Lord make his face to shine upon you, and be gracious to you; the Lord lift up his countenance upon you, and give you peace. (Numbers 6:24-26 NASB 1995)

The Legend from Numbers is Caleb

Caleb was in the Exodus with Moses, Aaron and Joshua. He was one of the twelve spies sent to scout the land of Canaan. He gave an honest report, as did Joshua, and was granted entrance to the Promised Land. When Israel entered Canaan forty years later, Caleb was granted by Joshua the area around the City of Hebron for his faithfulness.

The Legend from the Western Heritage Past Will Rogers

He was born in 1879, and gained fame from movies, personal appearances and his newspaper columns. He was known as the "Cowboy Philosopher" for his wit and wisdom from the Roaring 20's through the Great Depression and beyond. He was the son of a rancher who learned rope tricks, performed in vaudeville and Wild West Shows.

Rogers ran away from his wealthy father and became a cowboy on the Texas Panhandle. Then later sailed to Argentina in 1902 and South Africa, where he performed in Jack's Wild West Circus as "The Cherokee Kid", a rope artist and bronco buster. He returned to the U.S. in 1904.

Rogers also appeared in the Ziegfeld Follies from 1916-25, at different times then moved to Hollywood where he became a star. His daily newspaper column was syndicated to 350 outlets and he wrote political commentary. He died in a plane crash in Alaska while traveling to Russia for a tour.

Quotes from Will Rogers:

"All I know is what I read in the papers."

"Everyone is ignorant, only in different subjects.

"It's great to be great, but it's great to be human."

"If stupidity got us in this mess, then why can't get us out?"

"Even if you are on the right track, you'll get run over, if you just sit there."

"I never met a man I did not like."

"Things will get better despite our efforts to improve them."

"If you injected truth in politics, then you would have no politics."

"We are so worried about the candidate if he is a Republican or a Democrat . . . we need to be worried about if they are any good."

"We show the world we are prosperous even if we have to go broke to do it."

"Things in our country run in spite of the government."

"We should not elect a President, we should elect a magician."

"I don't make jokes I just watch our Government and report the facts."

LESSON FIVE: DEUTERONOMY

"What does the Lord require of you, but to fear the Lord your God, to walk in all His ways . . ." Deuteronomy 10:12 NASB 1995

Deuteronomy pictures "Christ our Prophet!"
What does a long word like "Deuteronomy "mean? It means "second law." It is the retelling of the Law (the Big 10) to the second generation who will be going to the Promise Land. This book was written by Moses about 1405 B.C.

Moses Gives Three Farewell Speeches

First Speech: Chapters 1-4
In this speech he reviewed the history of the journey.

Second Speech: Chapters 5-26
Moses reviewed the "Big 10." It is like he reviewed the "operation manual" on what God wanted them to do. He instructed them about ceremonial, civil and social laws. He prepared them before they left for their journey to the Promise Land.

Third and Final Speech: 27-30
He positions the people around him and placed the leaders in the middle. He challenged them to obey God and told

them the results of disobeying God. He told them that they would possess the land and fulfill the plan and purpose of God. Chapters 27-28 tell about curses and blessings.

The Finality: 31-34
Here we have the Song of Moses and his blessings on the 12 tribes of Israel. He did not get to go into the Promise Land because of his disobedience. He went to the top of Mt. Nebo (Pigsah) and looked over into the Promise Land on the other side of the Jordon River. He then died and was buried by God.

Think and Apply
- We can learn from past failures.
- Why was Moses' grave hidden?
- Where does Moses appear again in the New Testament?
- The main law is summed up in Deuteronomy 6:5.

A Legend from Deuteronomy: Joshua the New Leader
As the Israelites left Egypt on their exodus, Joshua was one of the twelve spies sent by Moses to reconnoiter the land of Canaan. Joshua and Caleb were the only two who had confidence that God would give Israel the land of Canaan. Because of their faith God allowed Joshua and Caleb to enter the Promised Land but he vowed that the others of Joshua's generation would die in the wilderness. God instructed Moses to designate Joshua as his successor. Joshua led the Israelites into the Promised Land.

A Legend from the Western Heritage Past Bob Nolen
"He was born "Clarence Robert Nobles" on April 13, 1908, Winnipeg, Manitoba, to Flora and Harry Nobles. His surname was changed to "Nolan" when he rejoined his

father in Tucson in 1921. He was "Clarence Robert Nolan" or "Clarence" all the time he lived in Arizona. When he moved to California in 1929, his friends started calling him "Bob". He changed the order of his names when he started publishing music. ("Robert Clarence" made it simpler—it's always a little awkward when you are known by your second name.) He changed his birthdates to April 1, 1908 and his birthplace to New Brunswick simply by usage. He may never have known that he was born in Winnipeg. Dates, names and statistics were not important to him and he changed them freely to suit himself on documents. Music and poetry had priority in his life. Everything and everyone else came second. Nolan passed away on June 16, 1980."

Nolan was a founding member of the "Sons of the Pioneers" western singing group along with Leonard Slye (Roy Rogers) and Tim Spencer, and the group's original, but short-lived name was the "Pioneer Trio". Their first recording contract was with Decca records in 1934.

Nolan was a prolific songwriter and several of his most memorable tunes are *"Cool Water"* and *"Tumbling Tumbleweeds"*. In the mid 1930s, he and the "Sons of the Pioneers" signed with Columbia Pictures as helpers and tunesmiths for the Charles Starrett series. And in 1941, Nolan and the group saddled up at Republic to assist Roy Rogers.

It was during their days at Republic Pictures that the billing credit changed from "The Sons of the Pioneers" to "Bob Nolan and the Sons of the Pioneers". Nolan often had dialog and screen time as one of Roy's helpers/sidekicks. In the earlier films, it was Roy being assisted by George "Gabby" Hayes and Nolan, while the later entries featured Andy Devine and Nolan.

LESSON SIX: JOSHUA

" . . . As for me and my house we will serve the Lord."
Joshua 24:15 NKJV 1983

Y'shua, the name means "The Lord saves."

**Joshua pictures Christ as "Captain of our Salvation!"
Joshua was seen as a type of Christ.**

Author & Date
This book was written by Joshua and written: 1405-1385 B.C.

Moses & Joshua
Leadership had been passed from Moses to Joshua.
Joshua was now 80 years old and he led the Israelites to
the conquest of the Promise Land. The name "Joshua" was
originally "Hoshea", meaning "Salvation." Joshua finished
what Moses started.

Look at the similarities

Moses	Joshua
Passed through the Red Sea	Passed over the Jordan
Led Israel out of bondage	Led Israel into blessing
Gave a vision of faith	Led them into a walk of faith
Told them about inheritance	Led them into the inheritance
Anticipation from Moses	Realization from Joshua

Prepare (Chapter 1-5)
Mobilized the Army (Joshua 1-2)

The people of God were on the border of the land of promise on the banks of the Jordan. The people were anticipating the conquest of the land. Joshua's plan for success was spelled out in chapter one.

- Claim it—verse 1
- Take it—verse 2
- Move out—verse 2
- Believe God's word—verse 8
- Possess it-verse 11

Chapters 3-5: We see the people moving forward. They followed the Ark of the Covenant and passed over the Jordan. The main thing that we see is they believed and followed their leader, Joshua. In Chapter 4 we see the memorial stones that were set up so generations could look back and see the faith of the people of God.

Conquer (Chapter 6-12)
The first test was the fall of Jericho. The walls came down after the people walked around them for seven days. Rahab the Harlot, a resident of the City of Jericho, was a key player in this victory. She would someday be listed in the genealogy of Jesus Christ. She was also listed in God Hall of Faith in Hebrews 11. We see the Southern and Northern Campaigns where the people allow God to fight for them. We continue to see the Gibeonites and Canaanites defeated.

Allocate (Chapters 13-22)
It took seven years to conquer the land. It was time to allocate the land to the various tribes.

Final Words (Chapter 23-24)

Joshua gave his final words to Israel. He exhorts them to continue to love and obey God.

Learn from this

- You will always win when you let God fight your battles
- God uses people you would not think of using (Rahab)
- We have a choice in who we will serve
- Our prayers should not be that life would be easier. Our prayers should be that our faith may be made stronger.
- Look at chapter 14 and look at the great leader name "Caleb." It is said in verse eight that he "followed the Lord my God wholeheartedly."

The Legend from the Book of Joshua was none other than Joshua

- He was a type of Christ
- His influence: "And Israel served the Lord all the days of Joshua" Joshua 24:31
- The name *Joshua* is the Hebrew equivalent of *Jesus.*

Legend from Western Heritage Past Buffalo Bill Cody

Born: February 26, 1846
Died: January 10, 1917

William Frederick Cody, known as Buffalo Bill, was a buffalo hunter, U.S. Army Scout, and an Indian fighter. But he is probably best known as the man who gave the Wild West its name. He produced a colorful show called *Buffalo Bill's Wild West and Congress of Rough Riders of the World,* which had an international reputation and helped create a lasting image of the American West.

Buffalo Bill was a major contributor in the creation of the myth of the American West, as seen in Hollywood movies and television.

Lesson Seven: Judges

"Another generation arose after them who did not know the Lord." Judges 2:10 NKJV 1983

Judges pictures "Christ the Delivering Judge!"
This book was authored by Samuel and was probably written around 1043 B.C.

Judges is a diary of decline.

It Covers
Judges opens with the life of Joshua and continues to the ascension of Saul, the first King of Israel.

Purpose of the Book
The Book of Judges was written to defend the origin of the kingship in Israel by showing the tragic decline of Israel.

Caution
"Everyone did as he saw right in his own eyes." Judges 17:6 (this phrase runs through the last five chapters of Judges)

Failure: Chapters 1-2
The first two chapters tell about the Military failures of Israel after the death of Joshua. The people of Israel compromised God's command to get rid of the godless

inhabitants. The decision to disobey God would cause them misery because of the godless inhabitants.

The Oppression of Judges: Chapters (3-16)
The pattern of idolatry, oppression, and a brief deliverance described at the end of chapter two is described in chapters 3-16.

In these chapters there are seven different Judges for Israel. In the Book of Judges there are 114 years of oppression and 296 years of peace.

Interesting Finds
- Deborah, the only female judge. (Judges 4-5)
- Gideon and his 300 men. (Judges 7:1-7)
- Samson & Delilah. (Judges 16:4-22)
- Israel and the tribe of Benjamin. (Judges 20)

A Sad Commentary of Israel
"In those days there was no king in Israel; everyone did what was right in his own eyes." (Judges 21:25)

Life Lessons from Judges
1. Compromise leads to defeat.
2. The effects of disobeying God.
3. Don't put off in asking God for help.
4. Don't do what is right in your eyes—do what is right in God's eyes.

One of the Legends from Judges:
Gideon "he who cast down"
Gideon was the son of Joash the Abiezrite from Ophrah. He was Israel's fourth major Judge after the birth of Joshua. A

large army of Midianites and other nations united against Israel. The Lord told Gideon that he would be made strong and that he was to save Israel from the Midianites.

Gideon raised an army of 32,000 but after several test by the Lord the army was whittled down to 300 men. God did this so the people of Israel would not boast to Him that they saved themselves by their own strength. At night Gideon and his 300 men lit torches, blew trumpets, and shouted *"For the Lord and for Gideon."* Then they stood by and watched as the enemy panicked and the Lord caused the enemy troops to begin fighting and killing each other.

Median never recovered and the land was at peace for 40 years during Gideon's lifetime. He returned home and had 70 sons by many wives. Gideon died an old man, and was buried by his father in Ophrah.

One of the Legends from the Western Heritage Culture: Judge Roy Bean "The Hangin' Judge!"

Of the many colorful characters who have become legends of the Old West. "Hanging Judge Roy Bean," who held court sessions in his saloon along the Rio Grande River in a desolate stretch of the Chihuahuan Desert of West Texas, remains one of the more fascinating.

According to the myth, Roy Bean named his saloon and town after the love of his life, Lily Langtry, a British actress he'd never met. Calling himself the "Law West of the Pecos," he is reputed to have kept a pet bear in his courtroom and sentenced dozens to the gallows, saying "Hang 'em first, try 'em later." Like most such legends, separating fact from fiction is not always so easy.

LESSON EIGHT: RUTH

"Your people shall be my people, and your God, my God." 1:16
NKJV 1983

Ruth pictures "Our Kinsman—Redeemer"
This book was authored possibly by Samuel and was probably written 1030-1010 B.C.

Ruth is a Diary of Redemption

Theme: This is a positive book describing the romance of redemption. It tells how Ruth, a widow of Moab, converted to the God of Israel and was redeemed by the kinsman of her late husband and mother-in-law, Naomi.

See Christ in Ruth:
- Boaz, the kinsman redeemer is a type of Christ.
- Boaz was related to Ruth through marriage. Christ is related to us by His incarnation
- Boaz was willing to pay the price to redeem Ruth. Christ was willing to pay the price redemption for us.
- Boaz took Ruth as his wife and Christ takes the church as his bride. (Ephesians 5)

Chapter 1: Ruth Renouncing

Ruth renounced her god and followed the God of Israel by following Naomi to Bethlehem. *"Your people shall be my people, and your God, my God." 1:16 NKJV 1983*

Chapter 2: Ruth Reaping

She volunteered to go into the fields around Bethlehem to pick up grain left behind by the harvesters. She met Boaz when she entered his field.

Chapter 3: Ruth Requesting

Boaz accepted Ruth's proposal.

Chapter 4: Ruth Redeemed

Boaz agreed to marry Ruth as a close relative and met the terms of being her kinsman redeemer. They had a son name Obed. Obed would become the father of Jessie and Jessie the father to King David.

Interesting Finds:

- The message of Ruth is that God will not fail or forsake you when you place your faith in him.
- Everything will work out according to His purpose. Romans 8:28
- Adverse circumstances are always an opportunity to demonstrate Godly character.
- Christ's lineage to Ruth.

One of the Legends from the Book of Ruth: Ruth

Ruth's liabilities: she a woman; she was a foreigner; she was poor; she was a widow. All this counted against her but she was helped by an older woman to overcome the difficulties she faced. She had the good sense to listen to the advice given to her by Naomi. The older woman was rewarded by Ruth's unfaltering loyalty. Her story illustrates the triumph of courage and ingenuity over adverse circumstances. She has special significance for Christians. In the Gospel of Matthew four women were included in the genealogy of Jesus (Matthew 1.2-17), and Ruth was one of the four.

One of the Legends from the Western Heritage Culture
Florence Hughes Randolph
DOB: Jun 1898 Augusta, Georgia
DOD: Apr 1971 Carter County, Oklahoma Year Inducted: 1994

One of early rodeo's illustrious female champions, Florence was born Cleo Alberta Holmes at Augusta, Georgia in 1898. Her daddy preferred the name Florence, the name she used her entire life. During the time Florence performed, she weighed only ninety pounds and was only four feet six inches tall. She was the first and only woman to master turning a backwards somersault from one horse to another

Ten—time World Champion Cowgirl Trick Rider and World Champion Bronc Rider, Florence made more than 500 rodeo appearances—bronc riding, trick roping, trick riding and roman riding. A petite woman, Florence was 13 before she learned to ride a horse and taught herself stunt riding. She worked in Wild West shows, raced motorcycles, doubled for movie stars and produced her own Wild West show, "Princess Mohawk's Wild West Hippodrome."

In 1971 Randolph told an interviewer somewhat proudly: "I've been carried off for dead several times." She was actually pronounced dead in the arena in 1923. Following another rodeo accident several years later she was rushed to the hospital, where she awoke to hear the doctor say that if she lived, she would never walk again. Alarmed, she jumped from the bed and fled the building clad only in a sheet! Article written by Sharon K. Hunt, Cowgirl Art

Florence won the converted Metro Goldwyn Mayer Trophy Made by Lambert Brother's Jewelers, 1927

This was the most prestigious and valuable trophy made for female rodeo contenders, this extravagant silver piece was commissioned by the Metro Goldwyn Mayer Studio in 1927 at a cost of $10,000. Honoring "Champion Cowgirls" at the Madison Square Garden World Series Rodeo, the coveted trophy was won by Florence Randolph in 1927.

1 AND 2 SAMUEL

The Establishment of the Kingdom

The Book of Joshua records the history of the children of Israel taking possession of the Promised Land after years of wandering in the desert with Moses. This high moment of victory and celebration was short-lived; however, soon Israel entered her darkest period of history as recorded in the Book of Judges. Israel forgot her covenant responsibility to the Lord God and the leaders during the period of the Judges. They were weak and ineffective in protecting Israel from her enemies. The pattern of Israel's history during this time was:

1. Apostasy—The people turned away from God and worship other pagan gods.
2. Judgment—God brought judgment on the people through oppression and war with her enemies.
3. Cry of Repentance—The people would cry out for deliverance.
4. Deliverance—God rose up a judge and deliver the people from oppression and war.

This period in Israel's history is summarized in the following verse: *"In those days Israel had no King, and every man did what was right in his own eyes."* Judges 21:25 NKJV 1983

Against this historical background, 1 and 2 Samuel recounts the story of Israel's development under the leadership of Samuel, Saul and David. During this time Israel was transformed from a group of loosely connected tribes under Samuel into a full monarchy in the late years of David's reign as King. The Lord God was to be King over Israel; however, 1 and 2 Samuel tells how Israel became like all other nations who had "earthly kings." The historical period covered in 1 and 2 Samuel is approximately 1050 BC until 950 BC.

Author

The author of 1 and 2 Samuel is unknown because the Books themselves give no indication as to his identity. The author probably wrote shortly after the division of the kingdom that followed the death of Solomon in 930 BC.

Theological Significance of 1 and 2 Samuel

The religious teachings and applications of 1 and 2 Samuel are important for us to understand today:

1. Political and military leaders are no substitute or protection from faithlessness and disobedience to the covenant relationship with God. God's protection was evident on Israel in the conquest of the Promised Land. But as the tribes settled into the land two great challenges arose from Israel's neighbors. The first came in the form of the false gods, Baal, Dagon, and Ashera—fertility gods of the nations surrounding Israel. These false gods led some to believe that Israel must worship these false gods in order to produce the crops needed for food. The second challenge came in the form

of strong military nations like the Philistines that fought and won victories over Israel who also professed loyalty to these false gods. To some these powerful nations suggested that the Lord God lacked the ability to protect Israel from the powerful armies and the power of their neighbor's false gods. Instead of remaining faithful to the Lord God, Israel wanted to be "like other nations" with a king and military leader. Israel forgot that living in righteousness and faithfulness to the Lord God was their only hope. Without righteousness, kings and armies could not protect the people. The lesson of Proverbs 14:34 NIV 1984 is demonstrated here:

"Righteousness exalts a nation, but sin is a disgrace to any people."

2. God's people must remain faithful to Him in victory and crisis. The stories of Samuel, Saul and David demonstrate that God is the Lord of history. God's hand is seen in the selection of Israel's leaders (1 Samuel 3:1-20; 9:15-16; 16:1), in His protection (1 Samuel 25:26), and in His judgment when God's people rebelled against Him (1 Samuel 15:35—16:7). Israel's defeat and oppression by her neighbors was not the result of the Lord's lack of power but rather the consequences of the people's disobedience to God's will. The call of God is to faithfulness and perseverance no matter the challenges we face:

"Therefore, since we are surrounded by such a great cloud of witnesses, let us throw off everything that hinders and the sin that so easily entangles, and let us run with perseverance the race marked

out for us. Let us fix our eyes on Jesus, the author and perfecter of our faith, who for the joy set before him endured the cross, scorning its shame, and sat down at the right hand of the throne of God. Consider him who endured such opposition from sinful men, so that you will not grow weary and lose heart." Hebrews 12:1-3 NIV 1984

3.   We live in a moral universe governed by God who is both merciful and just. The stories of Samuel, Saul and David reaffirm the foundational truth of our faith that God is the Lord of history and the Father of justice. David stands out in Samuel as an example of this truth. Although David was not perfect, he demonstrated his openness to God's leadership. As long as David was humble and open to God, he conquered Goliath, the Lord protected him from Saul's attempts to kill him, and prospered David as the King of Israel. Nevertheless, when David failed in sin with Bathsheba, and arranged for the murder of Uriah, judgment and rebellion broke out and plagued the final years of David's life as king. Israel's fortunes, whether good or bad, were not the result of a capricious and unpredictable god like the Philistines worshipped. It was the faithfulness or lack of faithfulness of Israel's people and their leaders that determined the destiny of the nation. This lesson is a reminder that while Jesus affirmed that God's blessings and misfortunes come to all people (Matthew 5:45; Luke 13:4-5). He also taught that based on faith in Jesus, the just and unjust would be separated for reward and punishment in the judgment (Matthew 13:47-50).

Background for Establishment of the Monarchy in Israel (1 Samuel 1:1-7:17)

The story of Israel's transition from twelve loosely united tribes to a centralized structure with a king begins with the rise and rule of Samuel. Samuel played an important role in the transition from the judges to the prophets who proclaimed God's Word. Samuel is the key to leadership in the selection of Israel's first two kings. Through Samuel the promises and responsibilities of the covenant became a part of the monarchy ruled by an earthly King.

The Call of Samuel (1 Samuel 3:1-21)

The call of Samuel came during a time of need for great spiritual light. Though Eli, the priest was faithful to God, his sons did not follow him and Eli failed to discipline his sons. Eli showed his character in recognizing that God was calling Samuel.

1. God calls a person to minister in His name (vs. 4-10). It is God who calls us and equips us for the task to which He is calling us. It is God's work in us as we respond to His calling.
2. There are no easy jobs in the Kingdom of God (vs.11-14). Samuel's first task was to inform Eli of God's judgment on his house for the unfaithfulness of his sons and Eli's failure to discipline them. If we do not counsel our family, someone will have to do it later (v.13). God always give strength to do the task we are called to do.
3. God blesses the one He calls (v.19). The Lord was with Samuel and continued to reveal His will and purpose to Samuel as he was established as a prophet of God.

The Establishment of Kingship in Israel:
1 Samuel 8:1-12:25

This section of 1 Samuel follows the rise of Saul as the first King in Israel and Samuel's role in anointing him King. Though Samuel is no longer the focus of these chapters, he plays an important role in reminding the King and the people that faithfulness to God is the only path to peace. There appear to be two views among the historical record of Samuel regarding the King and monarchy. One view is that the old tribal structure with God as King was preferred. The only failure in this organization was the people's lack of faithfulness to God who is the true head of Israel (1 Samuel 77:1-8:22; 12: 1-25). A second view was much more favorable to the monarchy. God himself would provide a King to deliver Israel from the hand of the Philistines (1 Samuel 9-11; 12:14-15). In the narrative history of the establishment of the monarchy, God demonstrates He is Lord of history and can use the events of history to accomplish His purposes as long as the people are faithful to Him. It is not the presence or absence of an earthly monarchy that determines the success of Israel; it is rather the faithfulness of the people to their covenant relationship that ensures the blessing and peace of God.

The Failure of Saul as King 1 Samuel 13:1-15:35

Saul met many of the outward criteria for being a King (1 Samuel 9: 1-2; 10: 23-24), but inwardly Saul lacked the leadership and gifts to meet the requirements of a King. He continually faced the military pressure of the Philistines and failed to follow the spiritual leadership of Samuel the prophet in keeping the commandments of the Lord. Saul was disobedient in following the guidance of Samuel the prophet (1 Samuel 13:12), he made foolish vows (1 Samuel 14:24-30), and displayed jealousy and poor stewardship (1 Samuel 15:13-25) until finally the Spirit of the Lord departed from him (1 Samuel 16:14).

David Replaces Saul as King (1 Samuel 16:1-31:31)

Saul had managed to create political and military power but had failed in his obedience and faithfulness to the covenant relationship as a representative of God in the Kingdom. As a result the Spirit of the Lord departed from Saul (1 Samuel 16:14), signifying God's rejection of Saul as King. God sends Samuel to Bethlehem to anoint the next King of Israel. Samuel is instructed to find a son of Jesse who unlike Saul possessed the inward gifts or character, leadership, and obedience (1 Samuel 16:8).

David and Goliath (1 Samuel 17:1-58)

In ancient time when one nation's army defeated another army, the victorious nation's god was believed to be stronger than the defeated army's god. The Philistines were continually challenging Israel and causing the people to doubt God's power to give them victory. One of the greatest challenges came in the battle between the giant Philistine, Goliath and David in the Valley of Elah. Goliath stood more than nine feet tall and his great size along with his intimidating call to the armies of Israel to fight or become servants of the Philistines caused Israel great fear. No one was willing to answer Goliath's challenge until the shepherd David, son of Jesse, answered the challenge. His story is a reminder that with God's power even those things that seem impossible become possible as expressed in 1 Samuel 17:26:

"Who is this uncircumcised Philistine that he should defy the armies of the living God?"

David was confident of God's victory because:

1. He knew he was equipped for the task (1 Samuel 17:34-35 NIV 1984). As a shepherd boy David had protected his father's sheep from lions and bears, and what David lacked in experience with military weapons he overcame in knowledge and experience with large animals.

2. He had faith in God (1 Samuel 17:27, 45-46). David knew that God was with him and had called him to the task. David did not just rely on his physical strength. He knew that God would provide for him the victory.

3. He knew God was the source for victory (1 Samuel 17:38-40). David could not wear the armor of Saul because it was not his gift. Some time we try to do the work of God through the gifts of others rather than the talent, knowledge and experience that God has given us. David used a sling and five smooth stones to stop Goliath. David wanted Goliath and all of Israel to know: *"All those gathered here will know that it is not by sword or spear that the Lord saves; for the battle is the Lord's and he will give all of you into our hands."* (1 Samuel 17:47). We are but God's instruments; it is God who gives the victory.

David Becomes King Over Judah and Israel (2 Samuel 1:1-8:18)

David became King over the Southern Kingdom at Hebron after Saul's death and later over all of Judah and Israel.

Israel continued to face conflicts with her neighbors and finally David was able to conquer the Jebusites who inhabited Jerusalem. He called Jerusalem the "City of David" and united the Northern and Southern Kingdoms. David moved the Ark of the Covenant to Jerusalem from Kiriath Jearim (1 Samuel 6-7:2), which symbolized the uniting of the divided Kingdoms politically and spiritually. David wanted to build a temple to recognize God's blessings and victories and to unite the people spiritually. Initially, Nathan the prophet approved David's plan (2 Samuel 7:3) but God reveals to Nathan that David would not build a "house" for God. God would build a "house" for David who will endure forever and whose throne will be established forever (2 Samuel 7: 8-16). The promise of an eternal heir to the throne is ultimately fulfilled in Jesus Christ.

David's Weakness and Failure as a King
(2 Samuel 9:1-20:26)

David had succeeded in uniting the nation and bringing a time of peace and prosperity to the land of Israel for the first time since God's promise to provide a home for His people. David faced his greatest failure at a time of great victory. The tragedy and destructiveness of sin is revealed in David's encounter with Bathsheba:

1. David's sin with Bathsheba occurred at a time of idleness. Instead of remaining faithful to his role as military and political leader, David sent Joab, his commander, to lead the armies of Israel while David stayed at home in Jerusalem (2 Samuel11:1).
2. Sin and temptation come to men no matter what their position and power. David should have been

busy in leading Israel spiritually, politically and militarily but in his idleness he gave in to temptation and committed adultery with Bathsheba (2 Samuel 11:2-5).

3.   Sin can never be covered up. David tried to cover-up his relationship by having Uriah, Bathsheba's husband, sent home from his military duty to sleep with his wife and cover up the fact the Bathsheba was pregnant with David's child. But Uriah was more righteous than King David; he refused to leave his post as a good soldier and would not go to his wife when all of the army was protecting the nation in tents (2 Samuel 6-11).

4.   Sin concealed will always multiply. When Uriah refused to go to Bathsheba, David first tried to get Uriah drunk. When Uriah still would not go to his wife, David had Uriah sent back to the front lines with instructions to have him killed. Sin always multiplies and results in the loss of consciousness of the consequences of our sin (2 Samuel 11: 13-27).

5.   The consequences of sin cannot be escaped. Nathan the Prophet confronted David about his sin. Nathan informed David that the result of his action would mean the death of his son and the continual conflict for his family and heirs (2 Samuel 12:13-14; 13-20).

Final Reflections on David's Reign (2 Samuel 21:1-24:25)
The final reflection on the life and rule of King David is summarized in 2 Samuel 23: 1-7. David is a model of the fact that God works His purposes in history in such a manner that men are left free to follow God's will

or to reject it. David demonstrates the potential best in mankind when in obedience he defeats Goliath and unites God's Kingdom. In stark contrast, David illustrates the worst in mankind when he sins and brings destruction on Bathsheba, Uriah and David's own family. The Books of Samuel richly illustrate that despite man's obedience and disobedience, God's power and will are sufficient to carry out God's purpose through the conflicts and choices of His people. We, like David, are entrusted with the freedom to choose and respond to God's divine leadership.

The Legend from 1 and 2 Samuel is King David:
David blazed the trail that established the role of the King and the nation of Israel. He had been set apart and exalted by the Lord, and when David remained faithful to the Lord he was the earthly representative of God for the people. When David ruled according to God's leadership, he brought peace and the whole nation a right relationship with God. When David was unfaithful, he brought sin and reproach on his family and the entire nation. Despite David's failures, God promised David an enduring line of ancestors to rule forever over the people of God, a promise that was fulfilled in a lowly manger in Bethlehem.

The Legend from the Western Heritage Past Charles Goodnight
Charles Goodnight was a cattle rancher in the American West, perhaps the best-known rancher in Texas. He is sometimes known as the "Father of the Texas Panhandle." Essayist and historian J. Frank Dobie said that Goodnight "approached greatness more nearly than any other cowman of history."

Goodnight was born in Macoupin County, Illinois, east of St. Louis, Missouri, the fourth child of Charles Goodnight and the former Charlotte Collier. Goodnight moved to Texas in 1846 with his mother and stepfather, Hiram Daugherty. In 1856, he became a cowboy and served with the local militia, fighting against Comanche raiders. A year later, in 1857, Goodnight joined the Texas Rangers. Goodnight is also known for guiding Texas Rangers to the Indian camp where Cynthia Ann Parker was recaptured, and for later making a treaty with her son, Quanah Parker.

Following the Civil War, Goodnight became involved in the herding of feral Texas Longhorn cattle northward from West Texas to railroads. This "making the gather" was a near state-wide round-up of cattle that had roamed free during the four long years of war. In 1866, he and Oliver Loving drove their first herd of cattle northward along what would become known as the Goodnight-Loving Trail. Goodnight invented the chuck wagon, which was first used on the initial cattle drive.

In addition to raising cattle, Goodnight preserved a herd of native—American Bison, which survives to this day. Many have followed the path prepared by Charles Goodnight, a true trailblazer for modern-day cowmen.

1 AND 2 KINGS

1 and 2 Kings are "His-story."
1 and 2 Kings, originally one book in the Hebrew Bible, tells the story of God as the sovereign Lord of History who uses people and nations to work out His redemptive purposes. Israel was God's chosen people through His covenant. From the time of Abraham and after the Exodus, Israel stood at Mount Sinai and entered into a solemn covenant with God (Exodus 19:5; 24:3-8). Israel was to be God's own people set apart from the nations, obedient to His commandments and loyal to Him. They were forbidden to enter into covenants with other nations and other gods. Adherence to the covenant with God would result in blessing; departure from it would result in cursing and judgment.

New Testament Application:
"You can't worship two gods at once. Loving one god, you'll end up hating the other. Adoration of one feeds contempt for the other. You can't worship God and money both." (Matthew 6:24) The Message

1 and 2 Kings trace the story of Israel's Kings from Solomon to the last King of Judah. This history records the sad story of the rejection of the covenant by most of the Kings. The Kings are identified and each King is compared with two Kings from Israel's past, King David who held

closely to the covenant, and King Jeroboam of Israel who forsook the covenant and caused Israel to sin against the Lord. David's parting advice to his son Solomon was that he should keep God's commandments (I Kings 2:3), which was the way to peace and prosperity. To depart from that way was to risk divine judgment. Israel's final collapse before Assyria (2 Kings17) and Judah's destruction at the hands of Babylon (2 Kings 25) was a demonstration and underlying proof of David's advice.

Author

The author of 1 and 2 Kings is unknown. He had access to three important records: the Book of the Acts of Solomon (1 Kings 11.41); the Book of the Chronicles of the Kings of Israel (1 Kings 14:19); and the Book of the Chronicles of the Kings of Judah (1 Kings14:19). The human author must have lived beyond the fall of Judah in 586 B. C. (*He recorded the release of Jehoiachin in 560 B. C. (2 Kings 25:27-30), because of his interest in the covenant and that he was a prophet contemporary with Jeremiah who wrote in the first half of the sixth century B. C.*)

The Reign of King Solomon: 1 Kings 1-11:43

David had grown old and was no longer capable of ruling as King. David gave sound counsel and guidance to Solomon to keep the covenant and to follow the statutes and commands of the Lord (1 Kings 2:3-4). Solomon remembered the words of David at the dedication of the Temple (1 Kings 8:22-66) reflecting the character and greatness of God:

- The Lord God cannot be contained in the temple or even in all the earth (v. 27)

- Hear the people of God when they pray (vv. 30-34)
- Forgive the sins of the people (vv.49-53)
- The Lord, Yahweh, is God there is no other (vv. 60-61)

Summary of Solomon's reign

It was the golden age:
- A time of peace
- A time of prosperity
- A time of great building
- A time of cultural achievement

Solomon failed to follow David's counsel:
- A time of great financial burden
- A time of unrest among the tribes of Israel
- A time of forced labor
- Solomon allowed the worship of foreign gods
- Solomon failed to keep the covenant

Israel Divides into Two Kingdoms:
1 Kings 12-2 Kings 17:41

The Kings of both Judah and Israel were passed in review and judged according to their faithfulness to covenant and whether they "keep the charge of the Lord your God to walk in His ways, to keep His statutes, His commandments, His ordinances, and His testimonies." On this basis very few Kings of Judah and Israel kept the covenant with God. Notable exceptions were Asa (1 Kings 15), Jehoshaphat (1Kings 22), Hezekiah (2 Kings 18-22), and Josiah (2 Kings 22-23), and even those had some defects. The faithlessness and disobedience of the Kings of Israel became a curse on the Northern Kingdom and resulted in the downfall of Samaria. This importance lesson is recorded in a sermon the author preached (1 Kings 17:7-18).

Renewal and Destruction:
The Single Kingdom Judah: 2 Kings 18-25:30

There was hope initially for Judah to learn from the disobedience of the Northern Kingdom Israel when Hilkiah, the priest discovered the ancient Book of Deuteronomy during repairs on the Temple. He took the book to King Josiah who calls the people of Judah to repentance (2 Kings 23). Josiah removed all the idols, idolatrous priests, shrines and altars to all foreign gods. The reforms did not last because the people only removed the external signs of idolatrous worship but failed to change their hearts toward God. The Kingdom of Judah failed when Nebuchadnezzar, King of Babylon destroyed Jerusalem and carried the people into exile.

The Prophet's Revolt Against the Wicked Kings:
1 Kings 17—2 Kings 13

Despite the faithlessness and disobedience of the Kings of Judah and Israel, God still had a faithful few obedient to His covenant and faithful to His commandments. The most important leader of the true worship of God since Moses and Samuel was Elijah, the Tishbite. The prophet Elijah is a reminder that God will always have a faithful servant and people, no matter how idolatrous and disobedient the leaders and people of the nation become. Israel had fallen into its darkest hour of idolatrous worship and abandoned the Lord God to worship the idolatrous nature god, Baal. Elijah stepped onto the scene as a spokesman for the Lord God (1 Kings 17-18). Elijah announced to wicked King Ahab that he and the people worship the "storm" god, but the Lord God declared there would be a drought until He gave the word that it would rain. For more than three years, as Elijah had prophesied, there was not a drop of rain until there were no crops and many animals were in great distress. In the midst of the great drought Elijah orders a full covenant assembly at Mount Carmel, including Jezebel's idolatrous 400 prophets of Baal. He called for a great contest between the false prophets of Baal and the Lord God to consume the altar on Mount Carmel to decide who was the true God (1 Kings 18:20-40). The Lord God consumed the altar after the false prophets of Baal were unsuccessful in getting their false god to consume the altar, and all the false prophets of Baal were destroyed. God demonstrated His power and greatness (there is no other god) through the faithfulness and obedience of his prophet.

Think and Apply

1 and 2 Kings remained as a warning to the people of God after the fall of Jerusalem, and it provided for them and for us today a practical lesson that rejecting God's covenant and failing to follow His commandments can only result in divine judgment. God chose Israel as his people to be a Godly nation and a light to all other nations for God. Israel forgot that her calling was not a privilege but a responsibility to serve God and to bring all other nations to a knowledge and understanding of the one true God. God offers us the gift of salvation through Jesus Christ who died on the cross to set us free from sin and judgment. But like Israel, we cannot forget that we are saved to serve and to become a light to all of the good news of Jesus Christ. Our service does not save us, Jesus does; but our faithfulness to God and our obedience to His word to be instruments of His love and grace in a world that is lost and without hope is a requirement for all who call themselves Christians. God calls us to remain faithful servants even if others choose not to follow.

God will have always have faithful servants who choose in the face of political pressure, peer pressure, economic, moral and personal uncertainty not to compromise and forsake God's promises and commandments for positions, power, prestige and prosperity. Like Elijah, there will always be servants who refuse to bow their knee to false gods. God's people will survive the unfaithfulness of political leaders, the attack of foreign conquerors, and even the apparent death of the nation. Nothing can ultimately conquer the rule and reign of God who offered Himself on the cross of Calvary. The King of all Kings lives today.

How can you serve God today? What barriers are keeping you from that service?

What are the most important priorities in your life?

What false gods do you need to confront in your life?

God calls us to choose to live in relationship to Him through Jesus Christ or to reject God and His offer of salvation. But we cannot serve two masters (Matthew 6:24). We must make a choice.

The one who says, I have come to know Him, and does not keep His commandments is a liar and the truth is not in him; but whoever keeps His word, in him the love of God has truly been perfected. By this we know that we are in Him: the one who says he abides in Him ought to walk in the same manner as he walked." I John 1: 4-6

The Legend from 1 and 2 Kings is the prophet Elijah

Elijah is a great example of a faithful servant to God, uncompromising in his faith and in his willingness to confront the faithlessness and disobedience of a disobedient nation. Elijah took an unpopular stand condemning the false gods worshipped by Israel and calling the people to repentance. He is a great example of how to be a faithful servant in a self-centered world.

The Legend from the Western Heritage Past Bill Pickett

Willie M. "Bill" Pickett was born in the Jenks-Branch community of Travis County, Texas. He was the second of 13 children born to Thomas Jefferson Pickett, a former slave, and Mary "Janie" Gilbert. The family's ancestry was African, white and Cherokee Native American.

Pickett attended school through the fifth grade, after which he took up hard ranching work. He invented the technique of bulldogging, the skill of grabbing cattle by the horns and wrestling them to the ground.

Pickett's method for bulldogging was biting a cow on the lip and then falling backwards. Pickett also made a living demonstrating his bulldogging skills and other stunts at county fairs. In 1905, Pickett joined the 101 Ranch Wild West Show that featured the likes of Buffalo Bill, Cowboy Bill, Will Rogers, Tom Mix, Bee Ho Gray, and Zach and Lucille Mulhall.

Pickett continued to work his entire life. He also served as deacon of Taylor Baptist Church. In 1932, he was kicked in the head by a horse while working horses at the 101

Ranch and died of his injuries 11 days later, at the age of 61. Will Rogers announced his funeral on the radio.

Pickett was named to the National Cowboy Hall of Fame in 1971 and was the first black honoree to that organization. He was enshrined in the Pro-Rodeo Hall of Fame in 1989.

1 AND 2 CHRONICLES

The Sacred History of Israel

1 and 2 Chronicles is a religious history of God's dealings with man from the time of Adam until King Cyrus, the Persian King, who released the exiled nation of Israel from the Babylonians in 538 BC. The record from the time of Adam to King David is presented in genealogies, which are primarily developed from earlier biblical records. The Books of Chronicles generally parallel Genesis through 2 Kings.

The Hebrew title for 1 and 2 Chronicles is literally, "things of the days," which means "things of the past" reflecting the focus in Chronicles on history. The English title for Chronicles is derived from the title that Jerome suggested, "Chronicles of the Whole of Sacred History."

1 and 2 Chronicles was originally one book in Hebrew. But when the Greek translation, the Septuagint, of 1 and 2 Chronicles was made it took twice as much space because the Hebrew did not contain written vowels like Greek. It became necessary to divide the Chronicles into two books, which is preserved in our English Bible.

Author

The author who wrote Chronicles is also believed to have composed the Books of Ezra and Nehemiah. Though there is some discussion and debate, most scholars believe Ezra was the author. The author clearly had great interest in and knowledge of the Levites and the ecclesiastical organization in Jerusalem. He had a passion for music and its importance in worship but he was also a prophetic interpreter of the rich history of Israel. He served as a great prophetic voice in a critical time in Israel's history.

Theological Significance of 1 and 2 Samuel

The primary purpose of the author of Chronicles was to provide a religious and theological interpretation of Israel's past to encourage the people after their return from exile in Babylon. His focus is on theological not chronological history. He reminds Israel of her covenant foundations of faith:

1. A Call to Faith. The Assyrians destroyed the Northern Kingdom of Israel in 721 BC. They would not allow the worship of the Lord God. When Jerusalem fell in 586 BC, the Temple was destroyed and all of the priests (sons of Aaron) were taken into captivity. The Levites were left to officiate the religious worship for the people left in Judah. When the exiles returned from Babylon there was great conflict with the people left in the land and the Levites were rejected as religious leaders. This ultimately led to the Samaritan crisis evidenced even during the time of Jesus (Luke 10:25-37; John 4: 1-26). The author of Chronicles was trying to correct this division and conflict that was the result of disobedience and failure to be true to the Lord God. Although Judah was the chosen nation of God all those from the Northern

Kingdom of Israel, the exiles from Babylon, and those that remained in the land (Levites) who desired to offer true faith and practice and sincere worship before the Lord God should be welcomed and accepted with open arms. True worship by the true people of God was what the nation needed to rebuild a right relationship with God.

2. God's Messianic Promise was still true. David was central to the author's religious view of history. It was David who wanted to build a "house" for God and while Solomon was the builder of the Jerusalem Temple, the Chronicler attributed the proper cultic observances in Jerusalem to David. Though the Temple no longer existed and the nation had been destroyed, the political nation needed to become a congregation where the promises to David could find fulfillment. God's promise of building a "house" for David was still possible if the people met the challenge and call to worship and service of God. All is not lost because the most important manifestation of the Kingdom of God was being expressed. God has called a holy people to faithfulness and through worship and service the ultimate victory of the Kingdom of God will be achieved.

3. A Call to Repentance. Although the author was concerned primarily with the practices and leadership of worship, he affirms the prophetic call for repentance. When the people of God listened to the prophets, they prospered; when they chose to ignore the prophetic word, they met disaster and defeat. Forgiveness and restoration are possible if the people will repent (2 Chronicles 7:14).

4. Learning the Lessons of History. The author reaffirms the lessons of history. When God's people are faithful to their covenant responsibilities, God blesses them. When they are disobedient, God brings judgment. Peace is better than war. God blesses His people with peace when they are true to Him. Wars are only necessary when men will not turn their hearts to God. Prayer, praise and worship are the true signs of the Kingdom of God.

Genealogies: From Creation to the Return from Exile
(1 Chronicles 1:1-9:44; cf. 1 Samuel 13-31)

The author of Chronicles was concerned to frame the history of Israel in light of the history of man. The national history was the culmination of the history of the human race. Each generation is seen as a part of God's plan for the nation and essential to finding meaning for those returning from exile in Babylon. By connecting Israel's past to the origins of man (the New Testament begins by tracing the genealogy of Jesus to Abraham; Matthew 1:1-17), the author gives Israel hope for a continued existence as the community of God after the exile.

The Reign of David
(1 Chronicles 10:1-29:30; cf. 2 Samuel 1-24)

With the nation of Judah in exile in Babylon, the Temple in Jerusalem destroyed, and no King from the line of David on the throne, the critical question before Israel was what about the promise of a Davidic dynasty? Did God's covenant promises still apply? Did God's promises to David have any relevance for a nation under Persian rule? The Chronicler answered the questions concerning the Davidic dynasty by showing the influence of David on

Israel's worship and cultic ritual. It was not his purpose to retell the history of David already recorded in Samuel and Kings. This history was primarily concerned with the prophets, Kings and chronological history of events. The Chronicler's goal was to highlight the religious leaders and priests and to answer the questions concerning the promises of God for the remnant of Israel.

The Reign of Solomon
(2 Chronicles 1:1-9:31; cf. 1 Kings 1-11)
2 Chronicles continues the history of David's royal line with the reign of Solomon. The focus of Solomon's reign was the building of the Temple and the worship of God. The hope of the returning exiles was to rebuild the Temple destroyed by the Babylonians. Israel's future hope lay in her covenant relationship with God. In repentance and worship Israel would realize the Davidic promises.

Temple dedication and Divine Response
(2 Chronicles 7: 12-18)
God's response at the dedication of Solomon's Temple was the same response and requirement for the returning exiles coming to rebuild the Temple and for us today:

1. Israel belonged to God. His name had been called upon the people. To be called by the name of God meant to reflect the character and nature of God. A name in the Bible was more than just a title; it meant to possess the nature and character of the one being named. (Simon became Peter; Matthew 16:13-18).
2. Humble submission to God. God requires nothing less than total surrender to His authority. Half-

hearted commitment brings destruction and judgment.

3. Prayer is the path to God's presence. Only through prayer can the people come into the presence of the Lord God (seek my face means to experience the presence of God).

4. Repentance is required. True repentance is a prerequisite to God's healing.

5. Forgiveness and healing are God's response when we approach Him in humility, seeking His presence, and confessing our sins. God can't heal what we conceal.

The Kings of Judah
(2 Chronicles 10:1-36:14; cf. 1 Kings 12—2 Kings 25)

The author of Chronicles focused his attention on the Kings of the Southern Kingdom Judah because when the Northern Kingdom rejected the Davidic dynasty, they ceased to be the true Israel. True Israel was to be found in the Southern Kingdom. He gave particular attention to the good Kings of Judah who remained faithful to God and favored the true worship of God: Asa, Jehoshaphat, Hezekiah and Josiah.

The Destruction of Jerusalem (2 Chronicles 36:15-23)

Chronicles concludes with the decree of Cyrus, King of Persia, who released the Jews from captivity under the Babylonians and allowed them to return to Jerusalem and rebuild the Temple. Despite the years of bondage, Israel still had hope as a people of God. Though military and political power had been absent for many years, there remained a shoot from the stump of Jesse that would come forth in true glory to God.

The Legend from 1 and 2 Chronicles is King David
See 1 and 2 Samuel for a discussion of King David.

The Legend from the Western Heritage Past
Joseph McCoy
Joseph McCoy was born in Sangamon County on 21st December, 1837. A farmer and cattleman, he purchased a small hamlet called Abilene in 1867. The name was taken from the Bible, means "city of plains". McCoy decided that as the area was good source of water and grass it would make a good place as a terminus for Texas cattle drives. McCoy built facilities for pasture and hospitality. After an advertising campaign, 35,000 head of cattle arrived in Abilene in 1867. McCoy also created the cattle trial to Wichita and played an important role in the Chisum Trial and other cattle routes. Joseph McCoy died in Kansas City, Missouri on 19th October, 1915.

EZRA/NEHEMIAH

"I was encouraged as the hand of the Lord my God was upon me." Ezra 7:28 NKJV 1995

"And the people had a mind to work." Nehemiah 4:6 NKJV 1995

Ezra/Nehemiah pictures "Christ our Restorer!"

Ezra: Return and the Rebuilding the Temple
> Date Written: 457-444.B.C.
> Author: Ezra

Nehemiah: Rebuilding the Walls
> Date: 424-400 B.C.
> Author: Nehemiah

Who is Ezra?
Ezra was a priest who led the return of God's people back to Jerusalem to rebuild the temple.

Who is Nehemiah?
Nehemiah was a cupbearer at the court of King Artaxerxes.

Unity
It seems that Ezra and Nehemiah is one book (Ezra-Nehemiah) in the Hebrew Canon

Outline of Ezra
Chapters 1-6: Return under Zerubbabel
Chapters 7-10: The Return under Ezra

Outline of Nehemiah
Chapters 1-7: Rebuilding of the wall of Jerusalem
Chapters 8-10: revival among the people of God
Chapters 11-13: The Reformation of a Nation

The Message
The Books of Ezra & Nehemiah cover 100 years of history. It starts in Persia and ends in Jerusalem. The two books center on the men who wrote the book. The theme of each book is the rebuilding of a nation and the rebuilding of God's people.

Interesting Note: Haggai was the main prophet in the day of Ezra, and Zechariah was the prophet in the day of Nehemiah.

Think and Apply
- Nehemiah was a man of prayer. Restoration and revival has to be birthed by prayer (2 Chronicles 7:14). Look at his prayer in chapter 9.
- What needs to be rebuilt in your life—Marriage, Relationships, Character?
- Nehemiah had a burden for Israel and the condition of his nation. Are you burdened about our nation?
- Ezra and Nehemiah were finishers. Is there something that you need to finish?

- Nehemiah had the gift of administration. Do you know what your spiritual gift is? Are you using that gift? (Romans 12: 3-8)
- You will never build the walls of your life until you have first become greatly concerned about the ruins.
- Ray Steadman said, "Don't despair—begin to repair."

The Legends of Ezra & Nehemiah in none other than Ezra & Nehemiah Ezra

The tradition is that the prophet Ezra wrote the Book of Ezra. It is interesting to note that once Ezra appeared on the scene in chapter 7, the author of the Book of Ezra switched from writing in the third person to first person. This would also lend credibility to Ezra being the author. Ezra which means ``help" was a famous scribe and priest who was the son of Seraiah and was probably born at Babylon. He was a scribe (teacher and interpreter of the Law) who went up to Jerusalem in B. C. 458 with the second body of returned captives. He spoke of himself as the author of the book which bears his name. It consists of two portions with a considerable interval between the two. The first describes the return of the captives in the time of Cyrus (536 BC), and the rebuilding of the Temple, interrupted by the Samaritans, but renewed at the preaching of Haggai and Zechariah

Nehemiah

God called Nehemiah to leave his service in the Persian king's courts and go to Jerusalem. He was sent to rebuild its walls which had been destroyed when Babylon attacked Judah and led them into captivity. Nehemiah allotted to every man a portion of the wall to build upon. "Arise and let us build" is the cry of Nehemiah and it is we who must heed this sound today. I am responsible for my portion of the wall that God allotted me and you are responsible for your portion of the wall. One plants and one waters is what we are taught In 1Corinthians Chapter 3. One man is responsible to lay a foundation in the lives of others and another is called to build upon that foundation

The Legend from the Western Heritage Past Wyatt Berry Stapp Earp

Wyatt Earp is best known for his participation in the controversial "Gunfight at the O.K. Corral," which took place at Tombstone, Arizona, on October 26, 1881. In this legendary Old West encounter, Wyatt Earp, his brothers Virgil and Morgan, and Doc Holliday faced off with Ike and Billy Clanton and Tom and Frank McLaury. The shootout and the bloody events that followed, combined with Wyatt Earp's penchant for storytelling, resulted in Wyatt Earp acquiring the reputation as being one of the Old West's toughest and deadliest gunmen of his day. Wyatt Earp would become the fearless Western hero in countless novels and films.

ESTHER: "As such a time as this . . ."

Key Verse
"So will I go in unto the king, which is not according to law; and if I perish, I perish." 4:16

Esther pictures Christ Our Advocate
This book was authored possibly by Ezra and was probably written 460 B.C.

Esther
The only Book of the Bible where you do not find the name of God, yet every page is filled with God.

Theme
Like Joseph and David, God used Esther for his purpose to the preservation of Israel.

Three Feast
The events of this book centers around three feast:
1. Feast of King Ahasuerus (chapters 1-2)
2. Feast of Esther (chapter 7)
3. Feast if Purim (chapter 9)

Outline
1. Esther becomes queen (1-2)

2. Haman schemes to kill Mordecai and damage Israel's hope (3)
3. Haman fails (4-8)
4. Celebration & Victory (9-10)

The Message of Esther
- What a crisis is to us is no crisis to God . . .
- Esther left all to gain all.
- Esther did not forget her roots and heritage.
- The deliverance of the Jews . . . (6-10)
- Haman: Pride goes before destruction."Pride goes before destruction, a haughty spirit before a fall." Proverbs 16:18

Esther a Legend of Israel
The fact that God placed Esther in a position that she could deliver her people, even before they were in danger, shows His far-reaching providence at work for His chosen people. This revelation would have been a great encouragement to the Jews of the postexilic period, as it has been to all believers since then.

The Legend from Western Heritage Past Dale Evans
Though Dale Evans is more famous for being married to singing cowboy star Roy Rogers, she is an accomplished performer in her own right. She was born Frances Smith in Uvalde, Texas on October 31, 1912. She spent her teen years in Arkansas and married at sixteen. The marriage was short-lived, however, and she soon embarked on a career as a pop singer. She sang with the Anson Weeks Orchestra, appeared on numerous radio programs, and held a regular spot on the CBS News and Rhythm Show. Dale Evans married Roy Rogers in 1947, and the couple

often appeared together on the big screen. Dale's film credits include "Orchestra Wives" (1942), "Swing Your Partner" (1943), "Casanova In Burlesque" (1944), "Utah" (1945), "Bells Of Rosarita" (1945), "My Pal Trigger" (1946), "Apache Pass" (1947), "Slippy McGee" (1948), "Susanna Pass" (1949), "Twilight In The Sierras" (1950), and "Pals Of The Golden West" (1951). Lately, Dale's work in music and television has been more in the gospel vein, and she's written many books of the inspirational type.

The Story Behind "Happy Trails"
"Happy Trails" was written by Dale Evans in 1950, while preparing for a radio show. Dale decided Roy needed a theme song and since he penned all his autographs with "Trails of Happiness" or "Happy Trails to You!"

An Added Verse of Happy Trails for Cowboy Church:

Happy trails to you, it's great to say "hello".
And to share with you the trail we've come to know.
It started on the day that we met Jesus,
He came into our hearts and then he freed us.
For a life that's true a happy trail to you.